Arkansas State Capitol

Little Rock

Jane Moorman

There is a saying, "It was a Friday night and it seemed like a good idea at the time." That sums up the beginning of the State Capitols Project.

When I told my brother of my idea of photographing state capitols, he said, "You do know there are 50 states and two of them you can't drive to."

Each capitol has its own unique beauty that reflects the state's personality when it was built.

Jane Moorman, photographer

Arkansas' statehouse

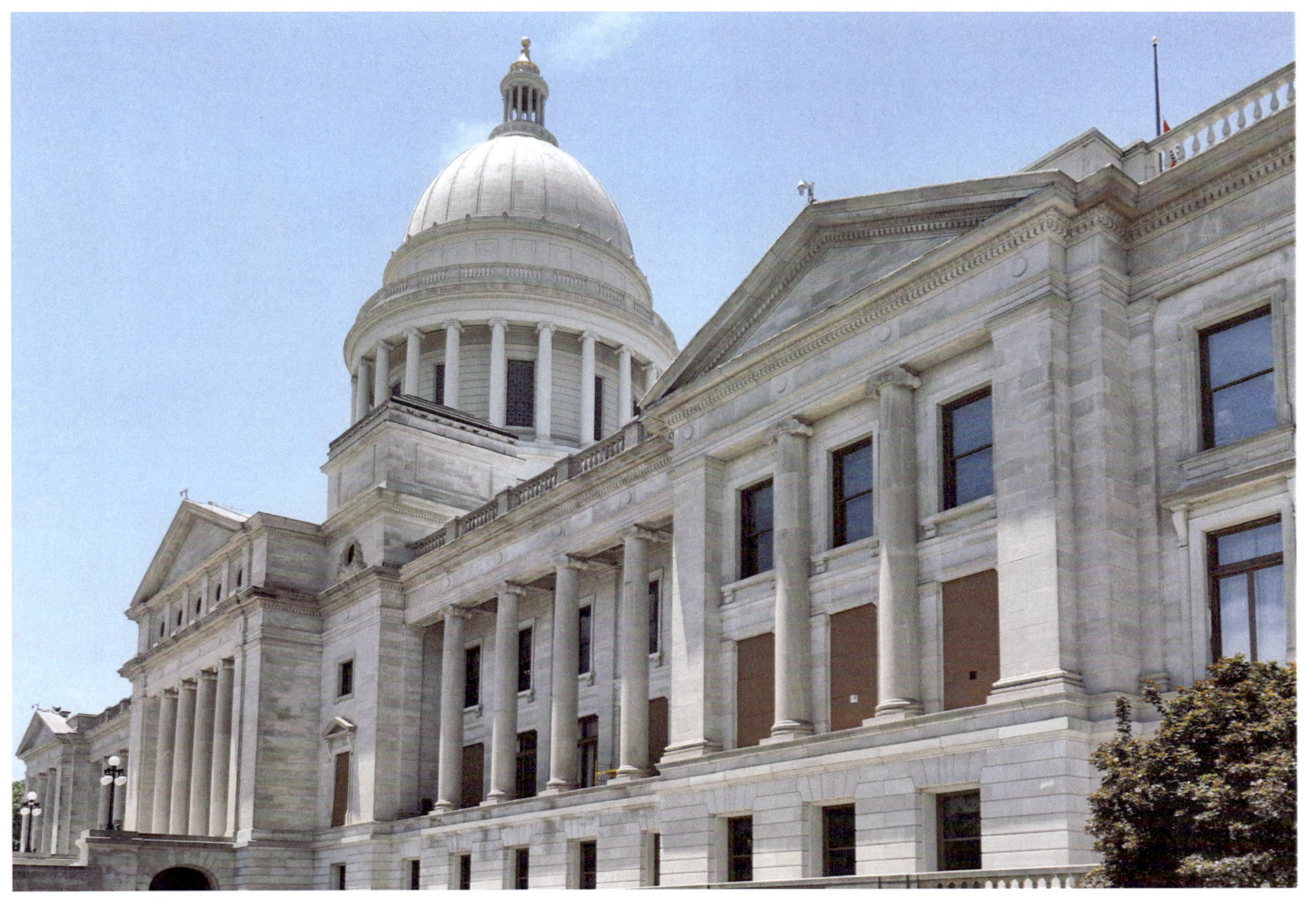

Arkansas' state capitol reflects the 15 years, 1899-1914, when it was built with its turn of the 20th century art deco motif.

The neo-classical revival style building was designed by St Louis architect George R. Mann. He supervised the construction from 1899 until 1909, when New York's Case Gilbert joined the project as supervisor to complete the construction.

Exterior walls are limestone quarried in Batesville, Arkansas. The interior is constructed of marble from three states -- Vermont, Colorado and Alabama. Paul Heerwagen designed the interior.

The stained-glass dome ceilings of the legislative chambers, along with the bronze grand entrance doors, elevator doors and mailbox are some of the unique aspects of the building.

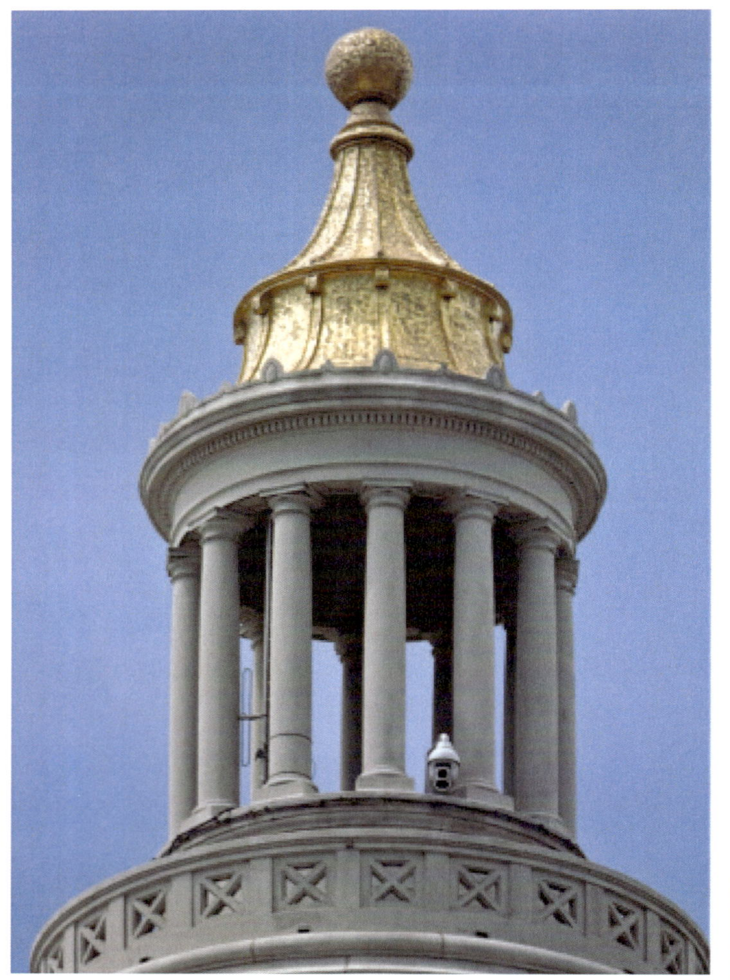

Capitol Dome

At one time, the dome was to replicate Saint Peter's Basilica in Rome, but it was changed to copy the stylishly spare dome of Mississippi's capitol.

Above the exterior walls of Arkansas limestone, known as Arkansas marble, rises the slightly conical dome built of softer Indiana limestone; 213 feet separate ground level from the top of the gold leaf-gilded lantern cupola.

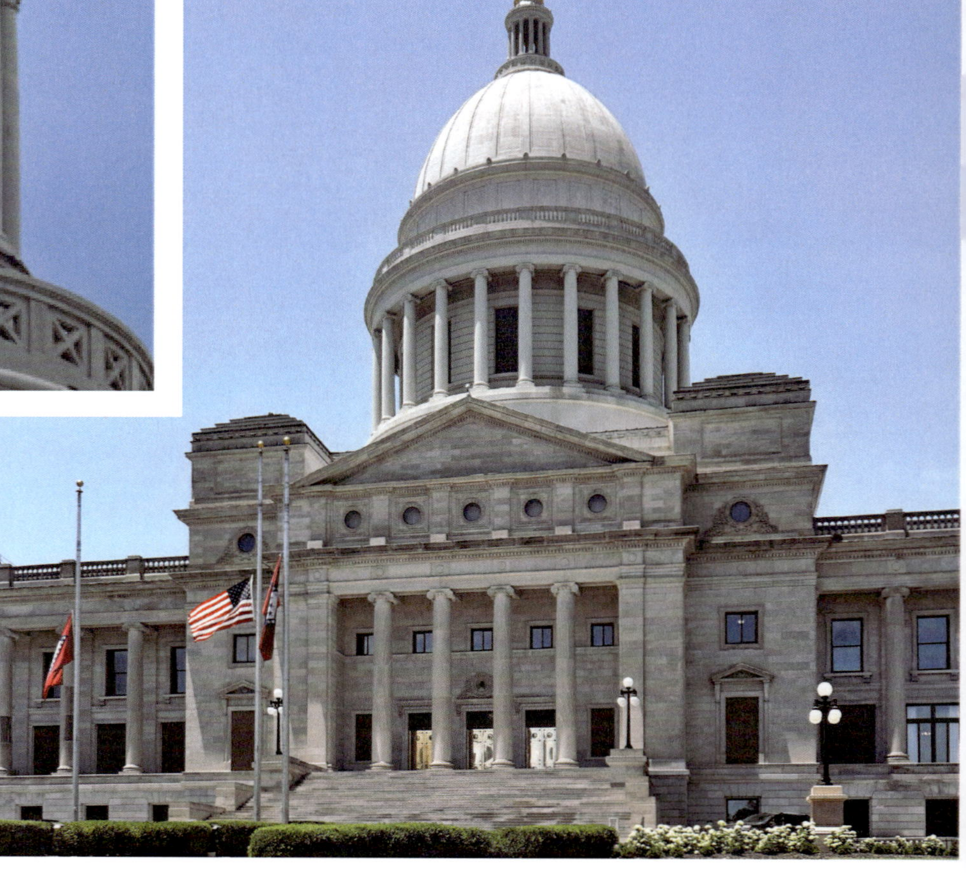

Hollywood Double

Hollywood producers have filmed movies at the Arkansas capitol and used it as a "stand-in" for the U.S. Capitol. Among the movie titles that featured it are 'Under Siege' and 'Stone Cold.'

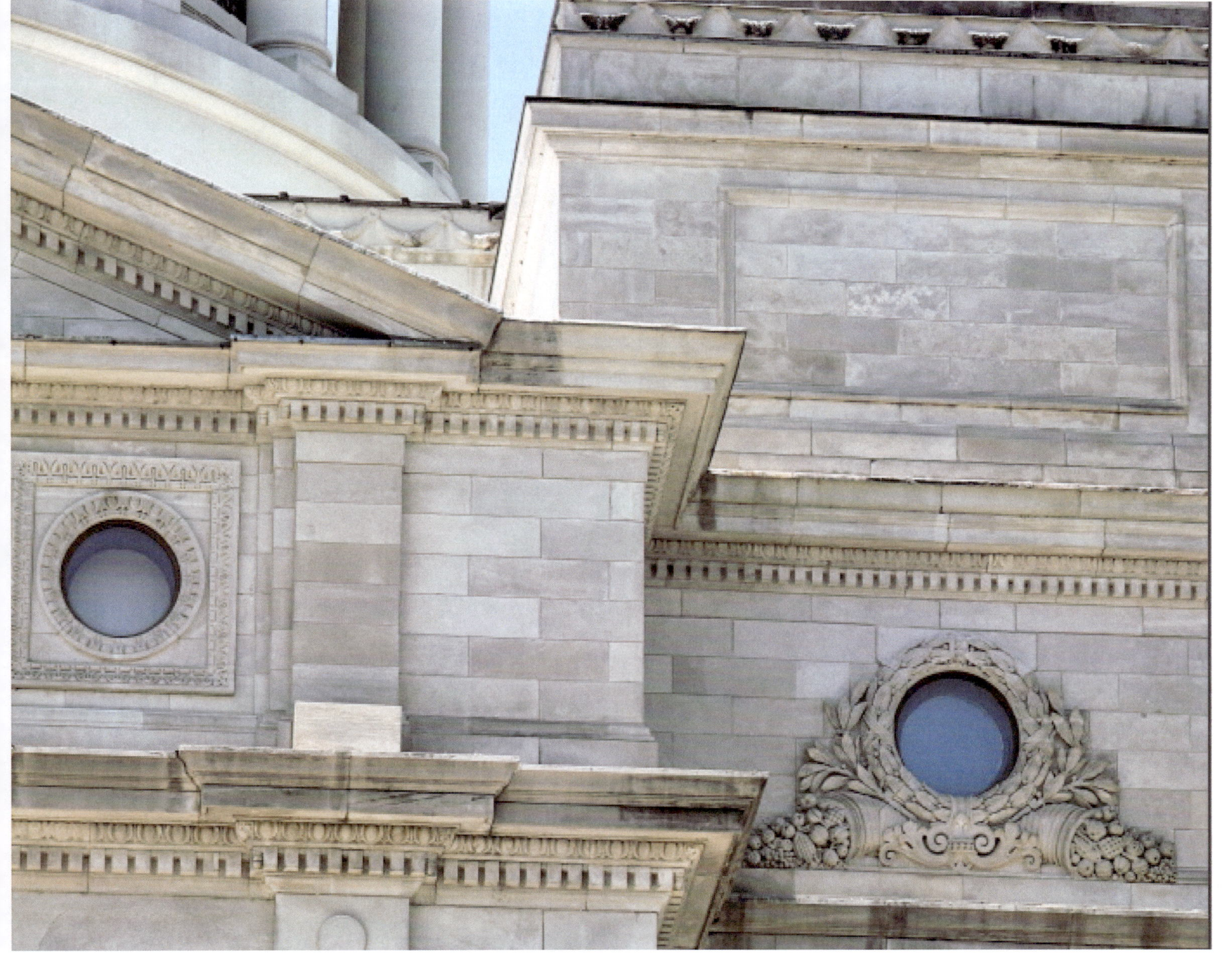

Elegant Building Exterior

Vermont marble with simple, yet elegant ornamentation highlights the windows, and the fascia of the building.

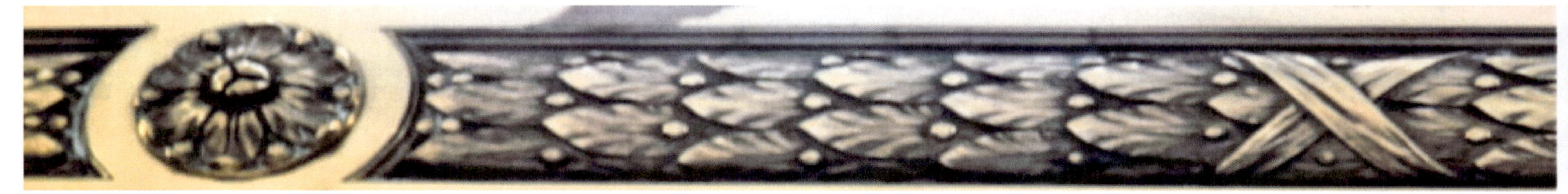

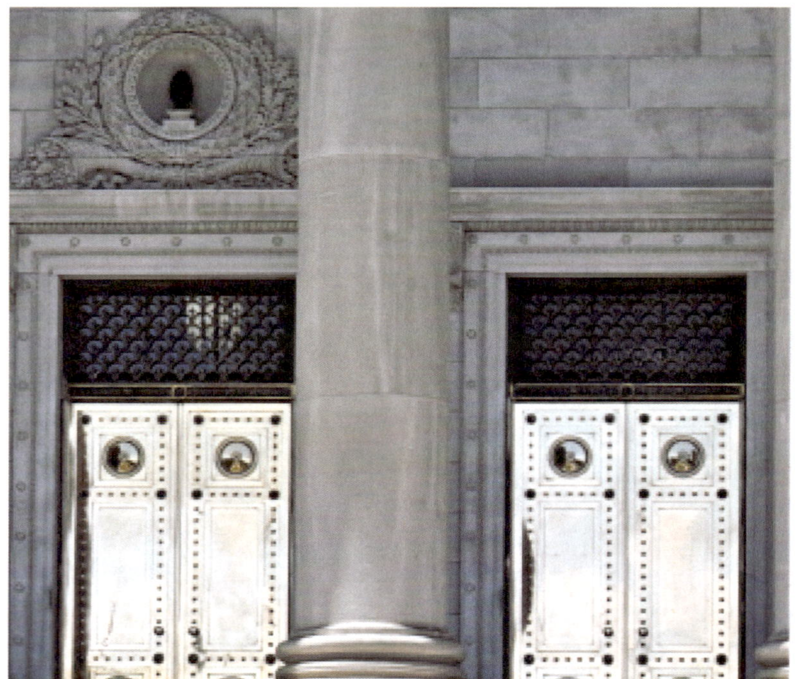

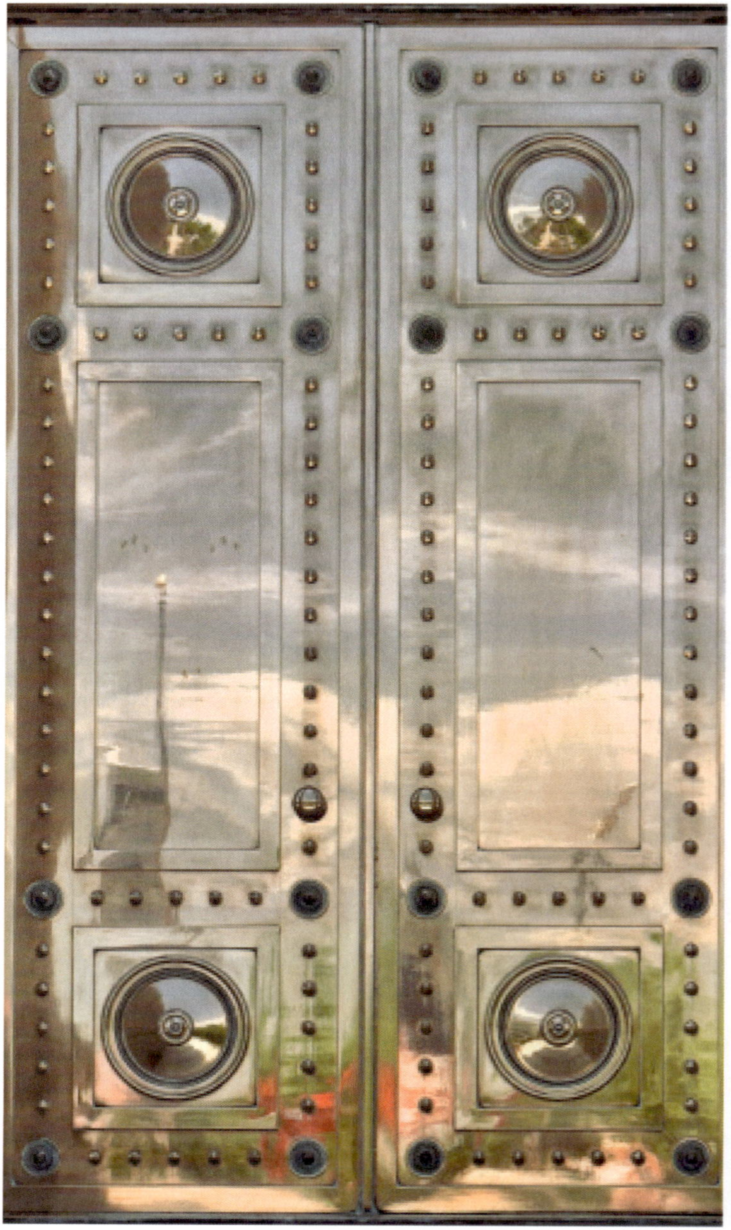

Grand Entrance

Three 10-foot-tall, four-inches-thick, polished bronze doors highlight the grand entrance at the top of 30 steps. The doors were designed by Cass Gilbert, and made by Tiffany Studios of New York.

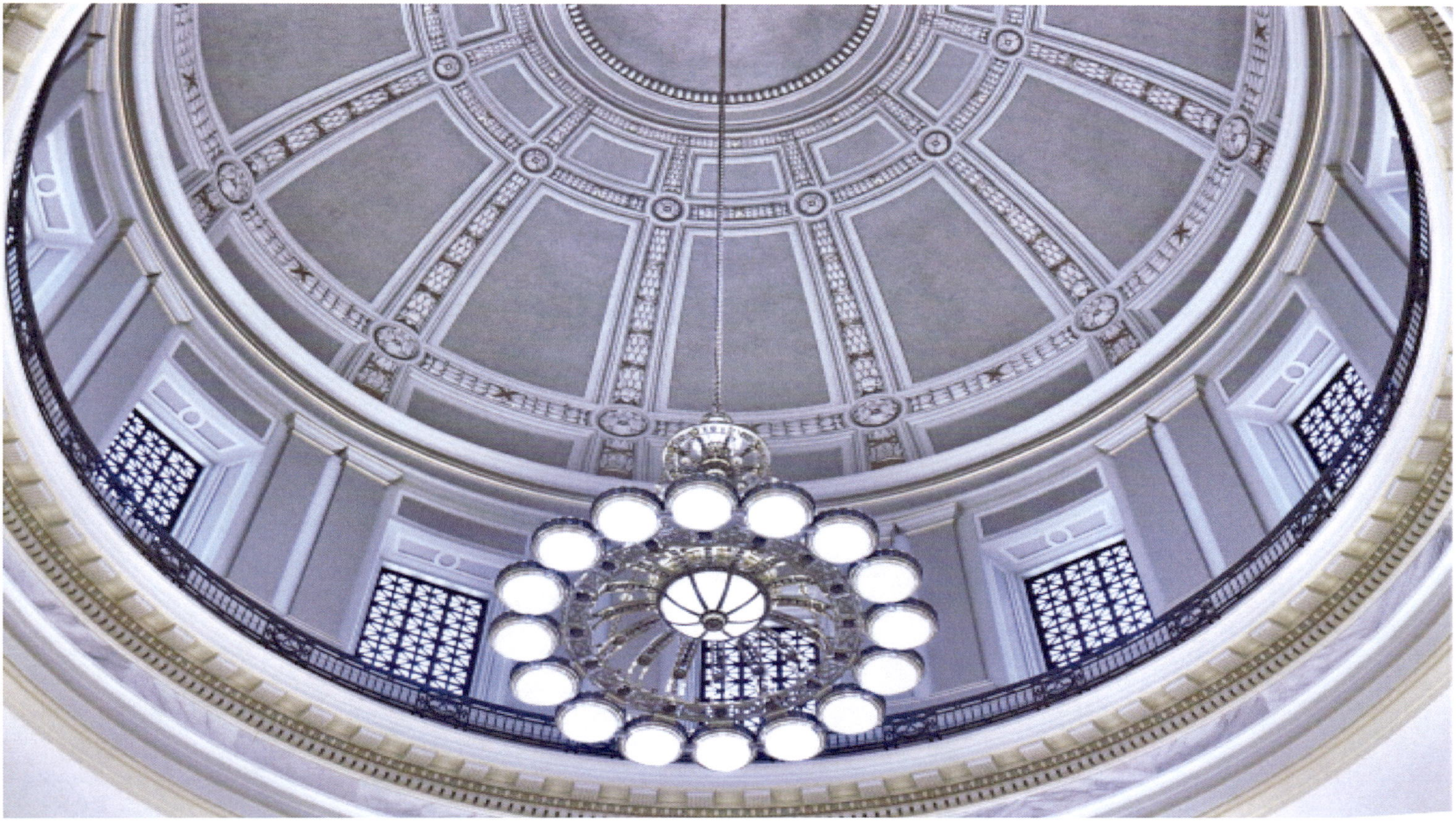

Rotunda Dome

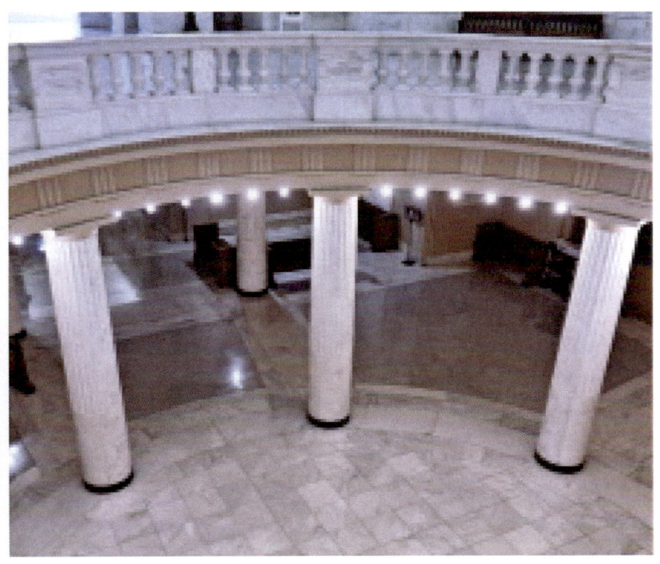

The dome's interior rises 160 feet above the rotunda first floor. Natural light from the windows circling the dome base illuminates the upper dome walls.

The 12-foot-diameter Tiffany brass chandelier hanging from the middle of the dome weighs 4,000 pounds.

The building's interior is constructed of marble. The floors and walls are Vermont marble. The third-floor marble columns are from Colorado. The marble grand staircases are from Alabama.

Rotunda Chandelier

An eagle rests on the top of the 4,000 pound chandelier which lights the interior dome and rotunda. The fixture is 12 feet in diameter and 18 feet in height. It is suspended on a 73-foot chain. The fixture fashioned by Mitchell-Vance Company of New York incorporates over two thousand brass, copper, zinc iron and glass parts.

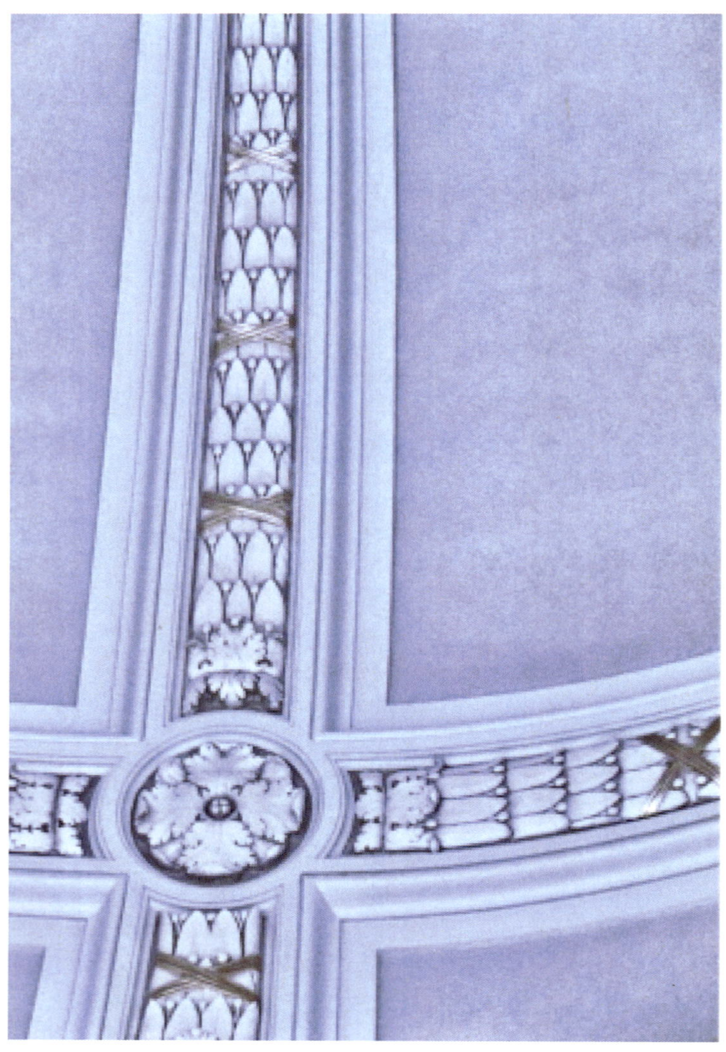

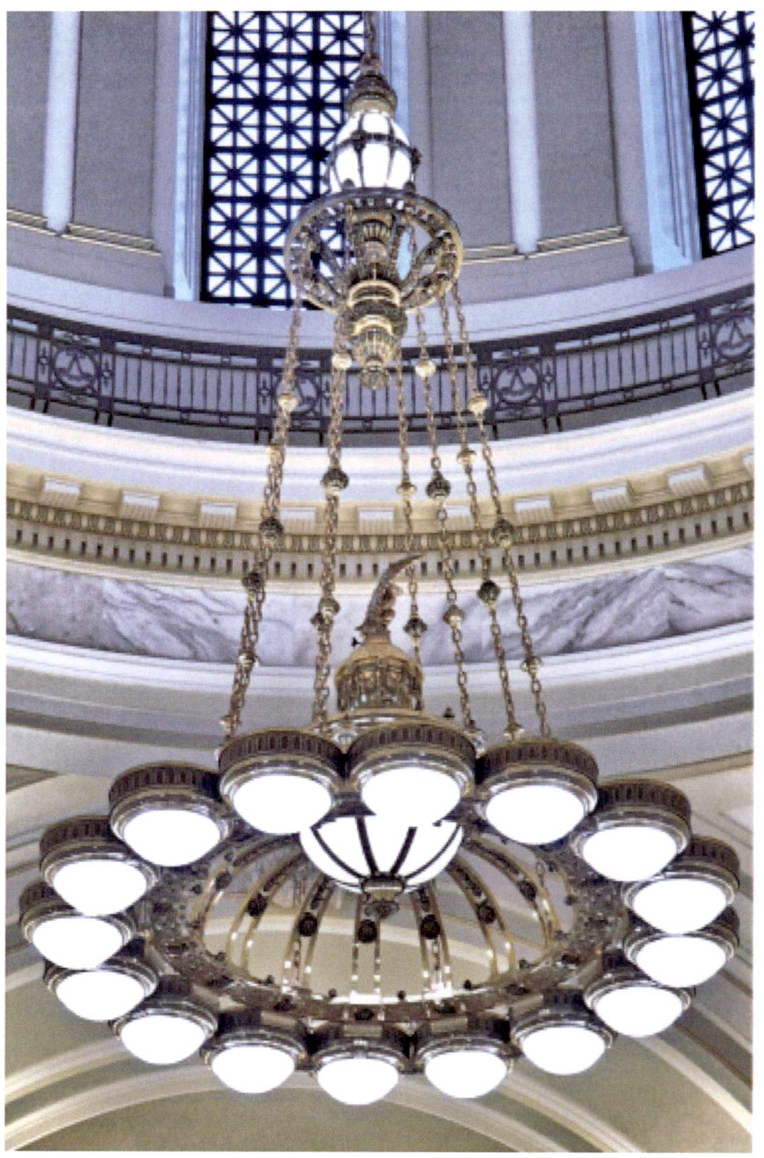

Dome Filigree

The interior dome is decorated with gold leaf highlighted filigree of flowers and leaves.

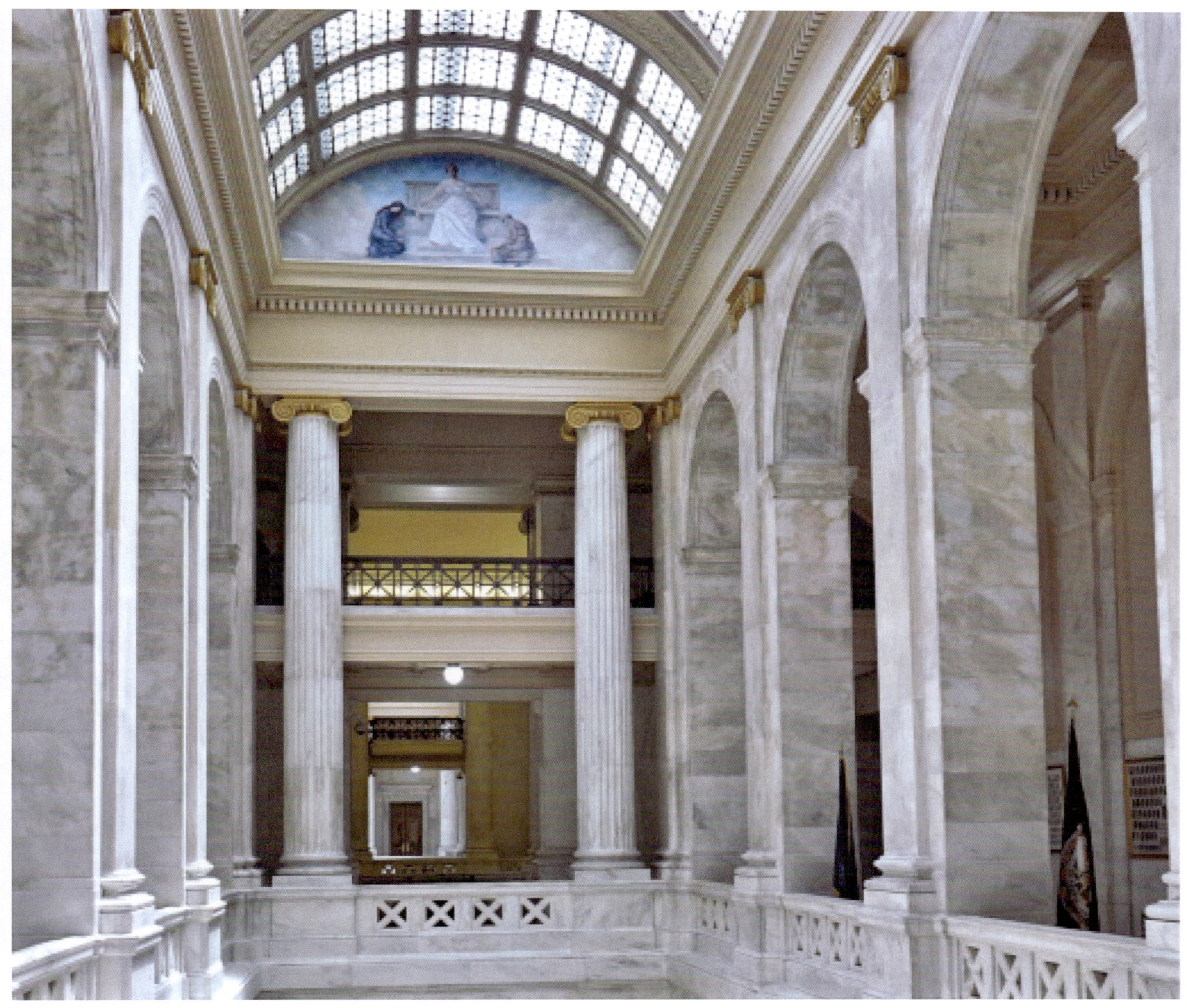

Grand staircase from the third-floor chamber to the second-floor rotunda.
Note paintings at the end of the ceiling.

Chambers Grand Staircase Lunette Murals

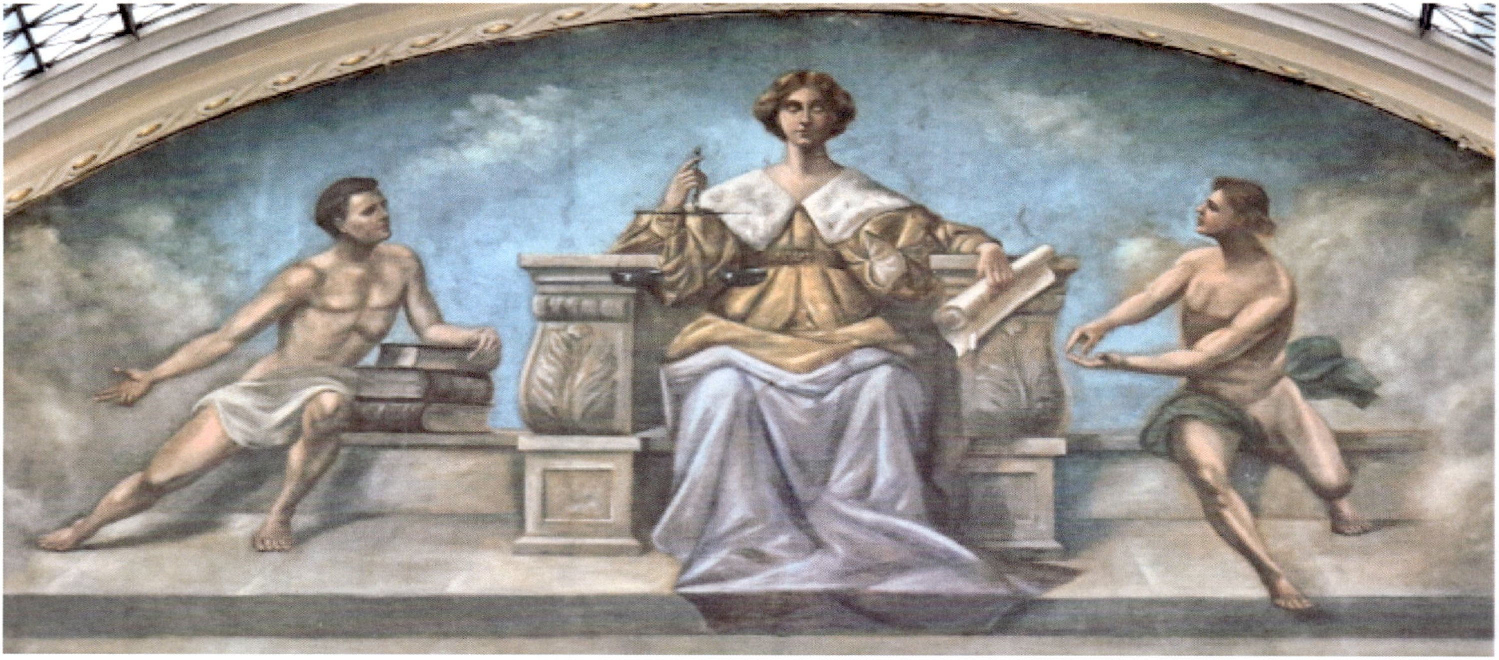

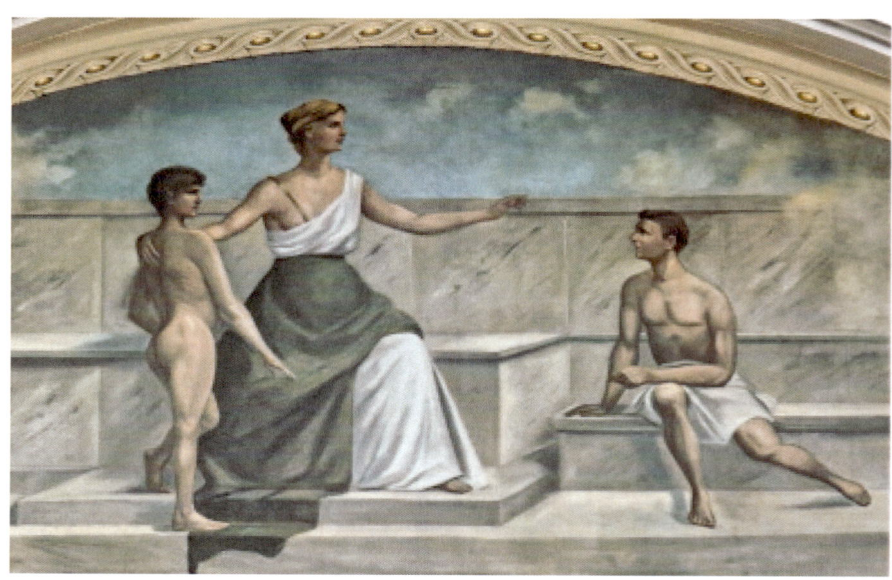

At each end of the glass-windowed barrel ceilings, above the grand staircases leading to the legislative chambers, are paintings designed by Paul Heerwagen, the capitol's interior designer.

He designed them in his Fayetteville studio, then shipped them to Little Rock for completion and installation. Some evidence suggests that artist Frederick Ruple painted the murals.

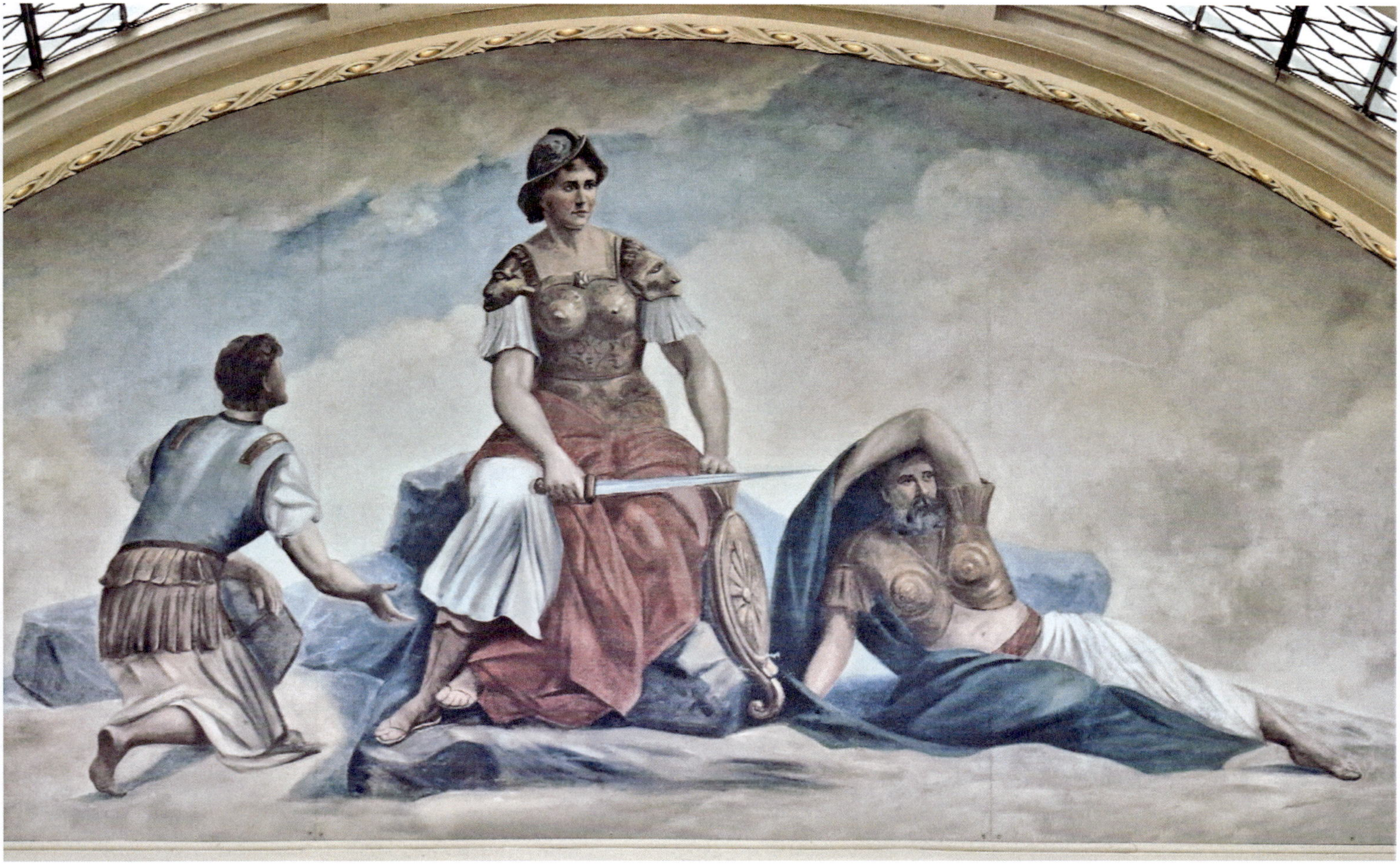

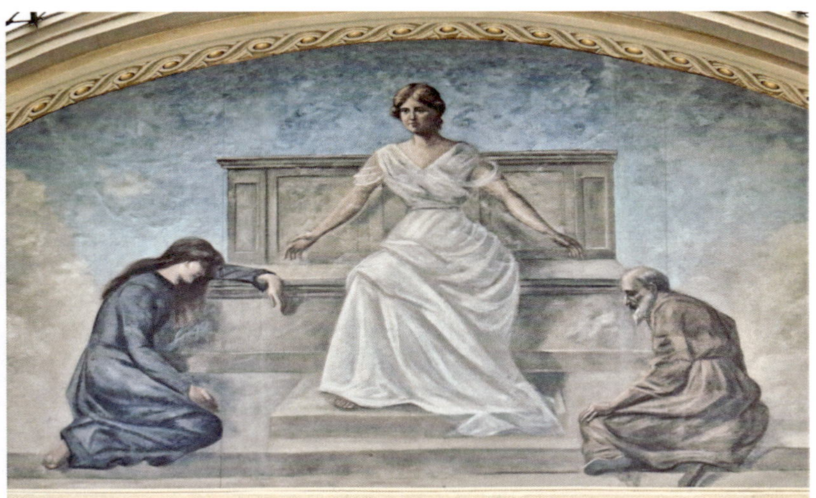

Left page

Top photo: Justice

Bottom photo: Education

Right page

Top photo: War

Bottom photo: Religion

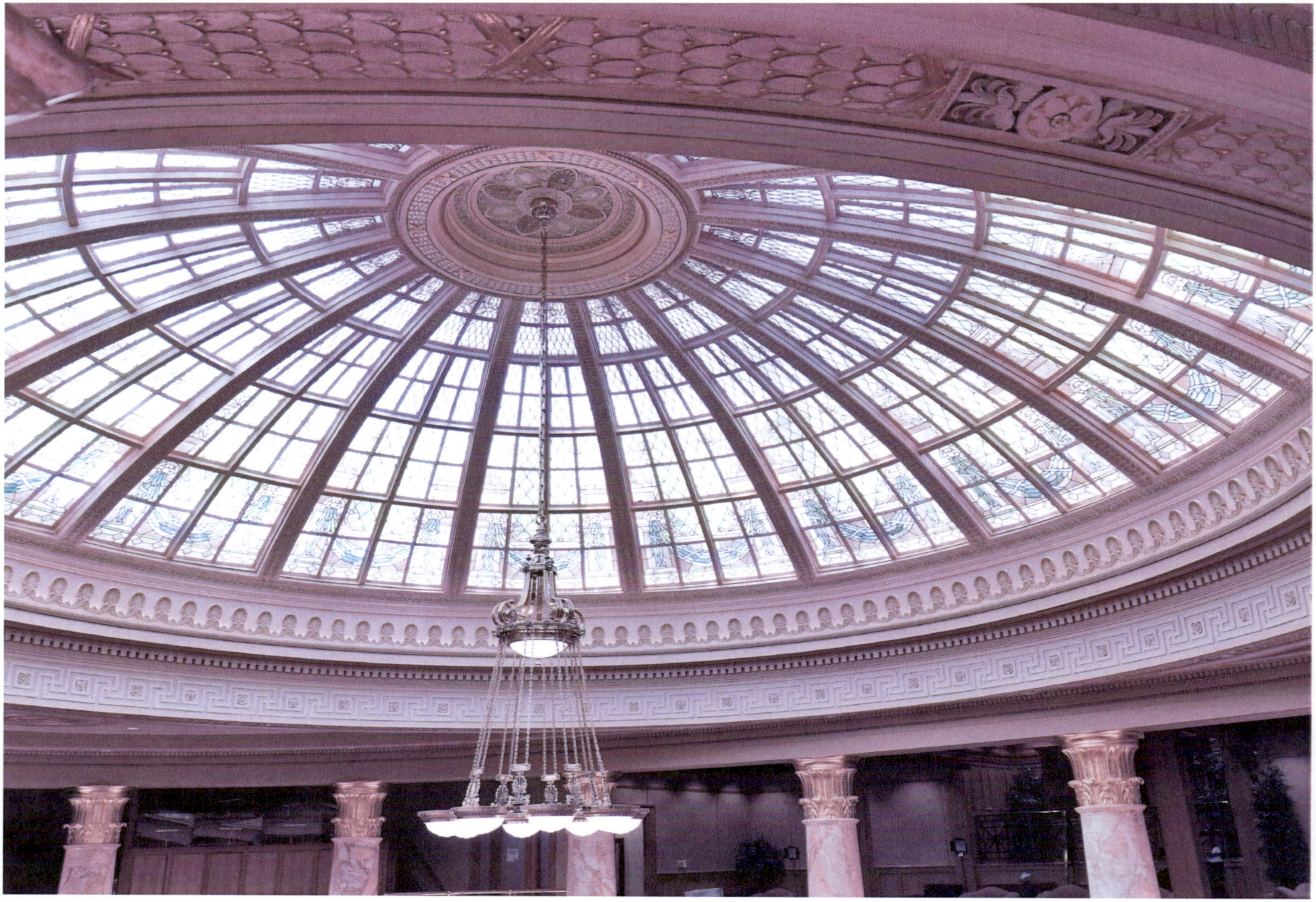

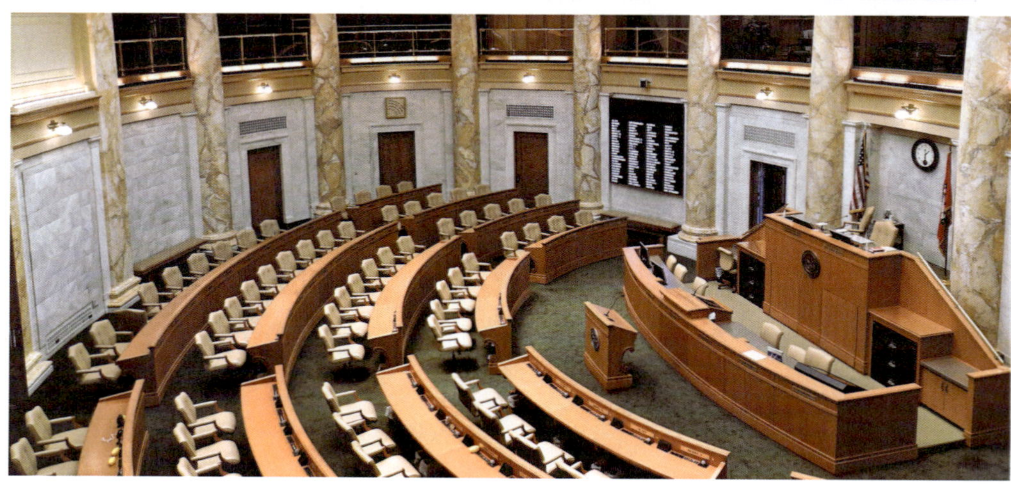

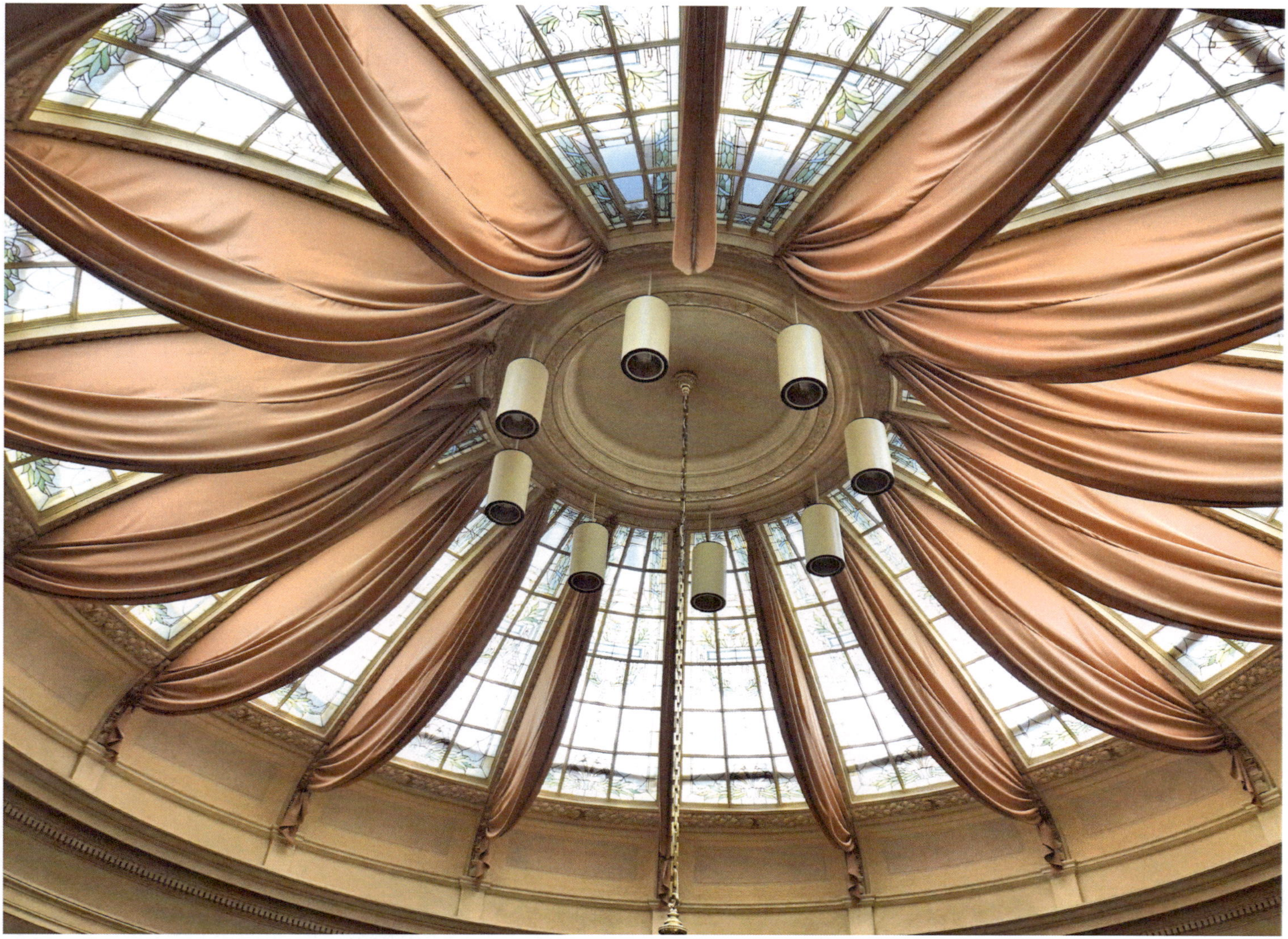

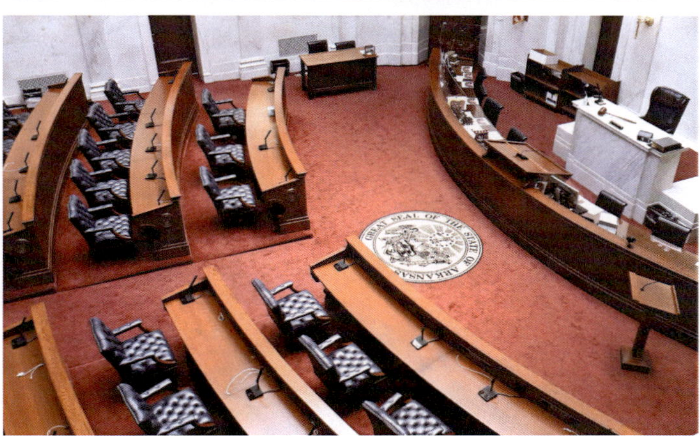

Chambers' Domed Ceilings

Ceilings of the legislative chambers are stained glass. Drapes have been added to the Senate ceiling to improve the acoustics.

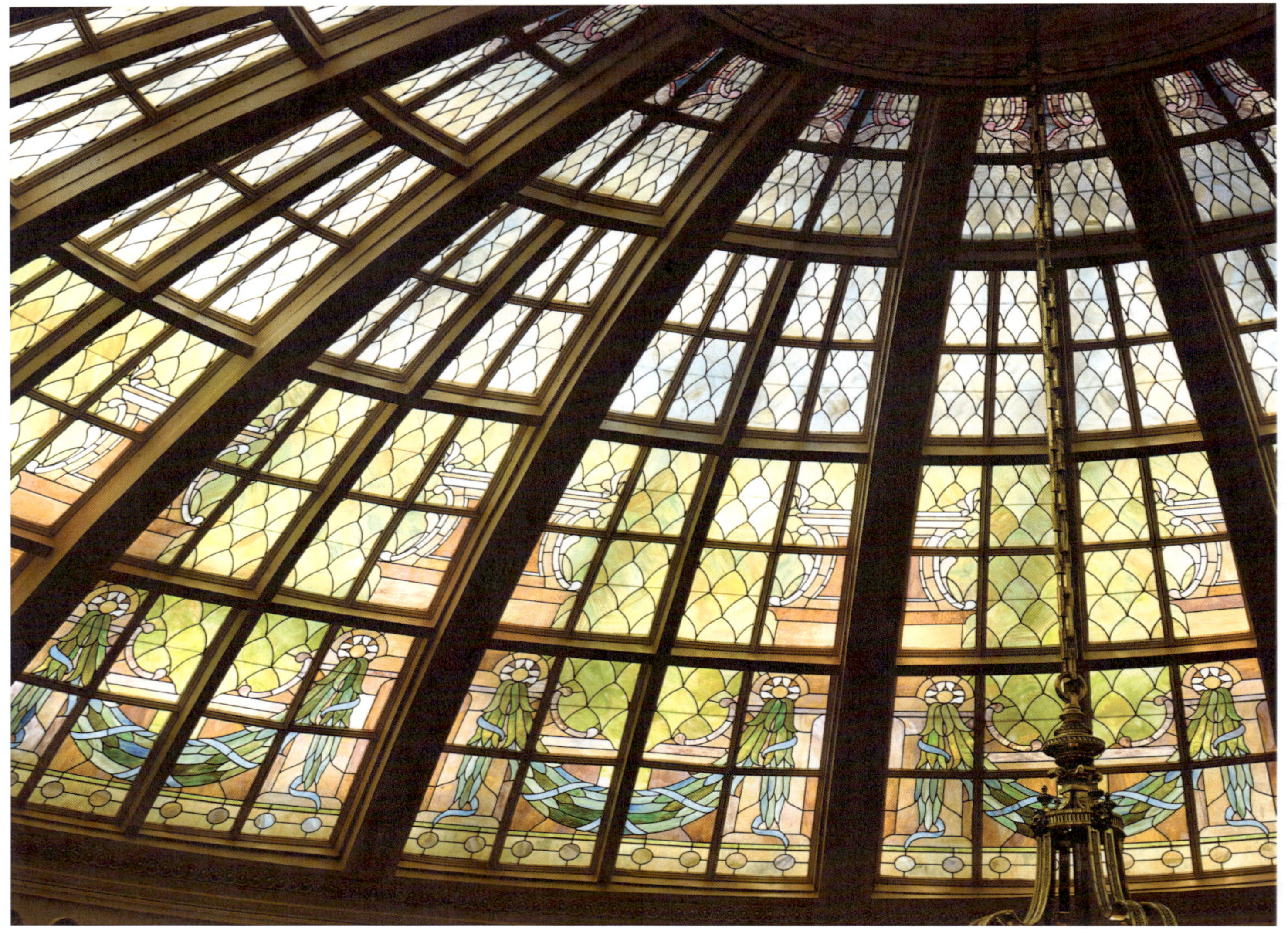

Stained-glass Designs

Legislative chamber ceilings have different stained-glass designs. Above is the House of Representative ceiling. Photo to right is the Senate.

The chambers also have different color schemes in their carpets - green for the House and red for the Senate.

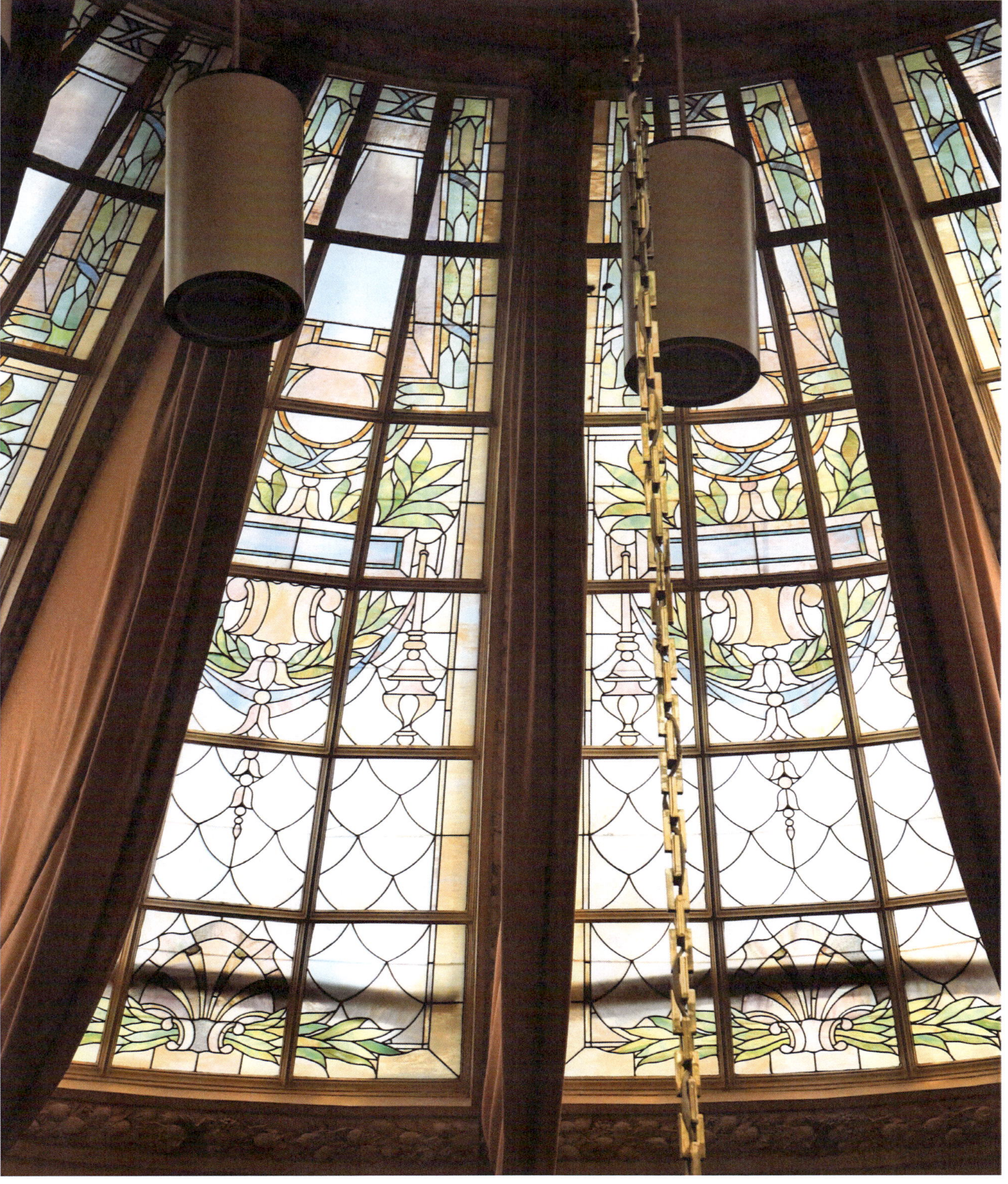

House of Representative Chamber Ceiling

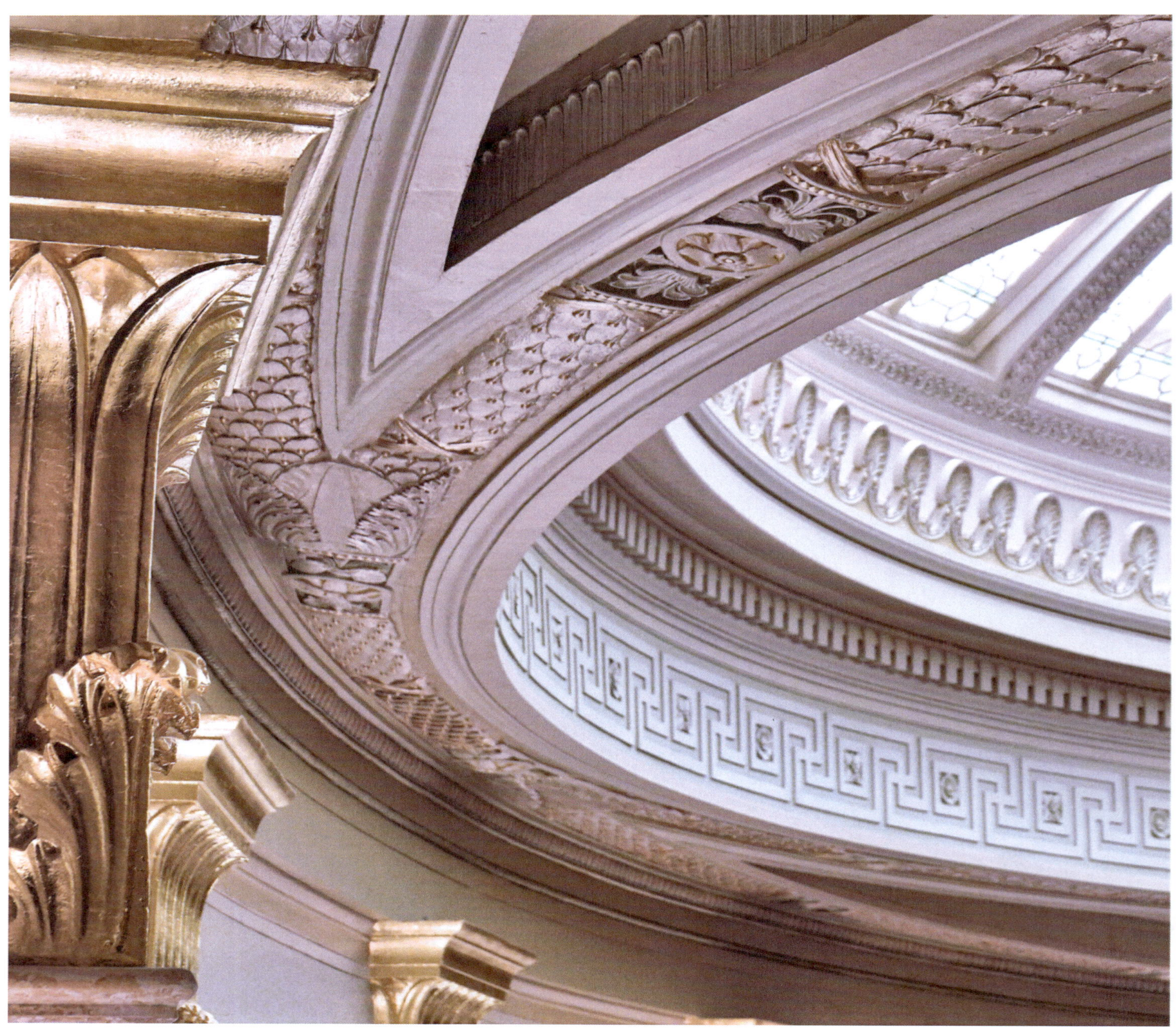

Chamber Details

Senate chamber doors are covered with pigskin leather.

Chamber column capitals differ. The Senate are ionic featuring volutes rolls, while the House are Corinthian.

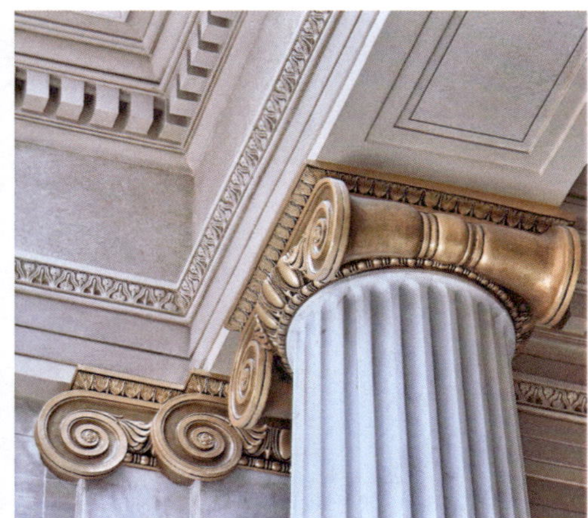

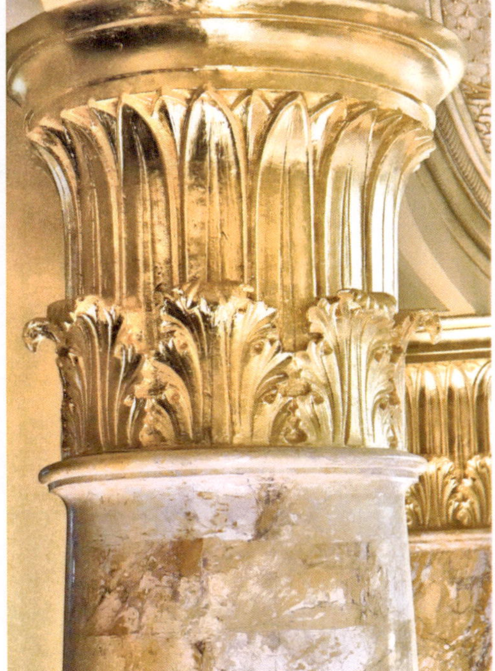

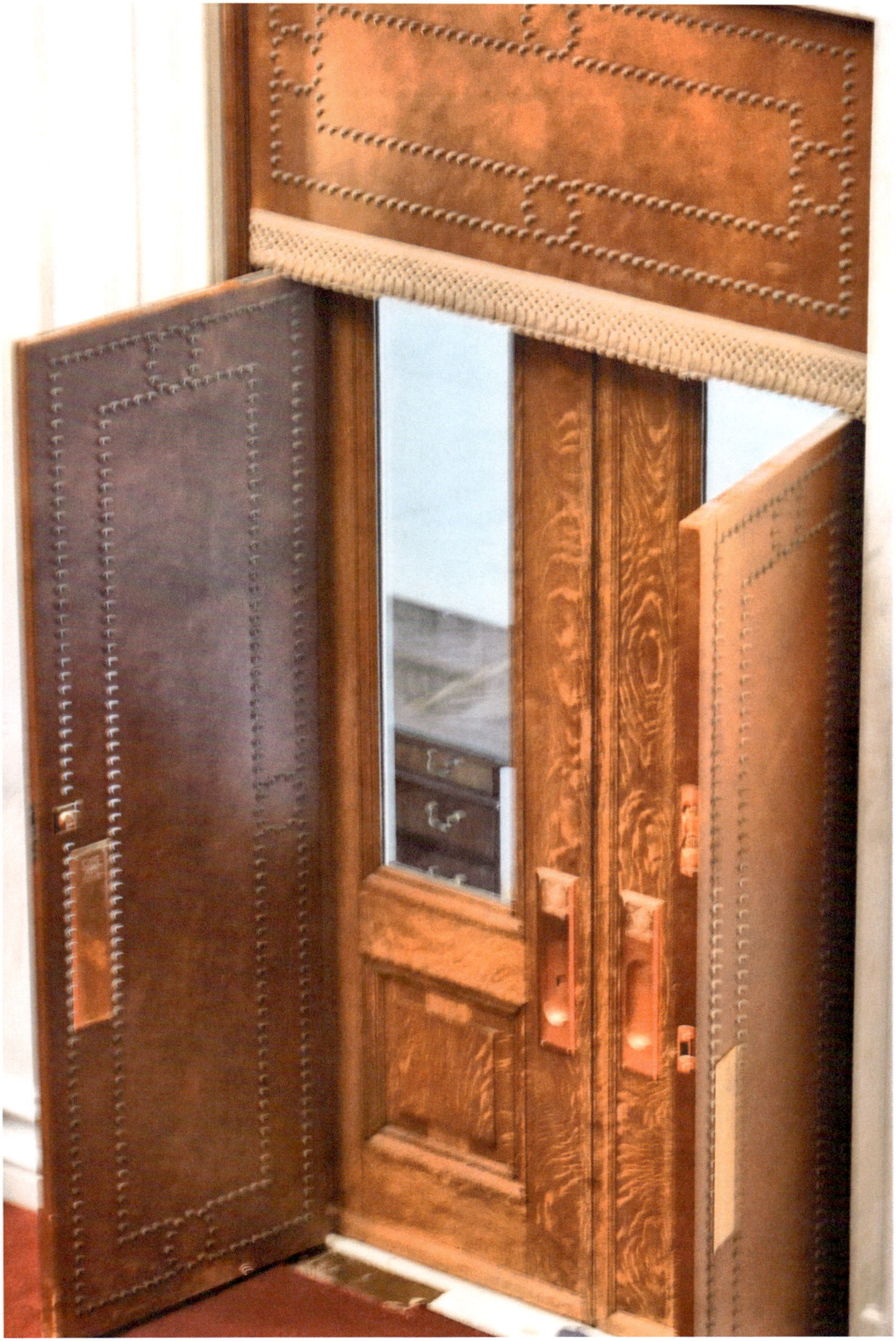

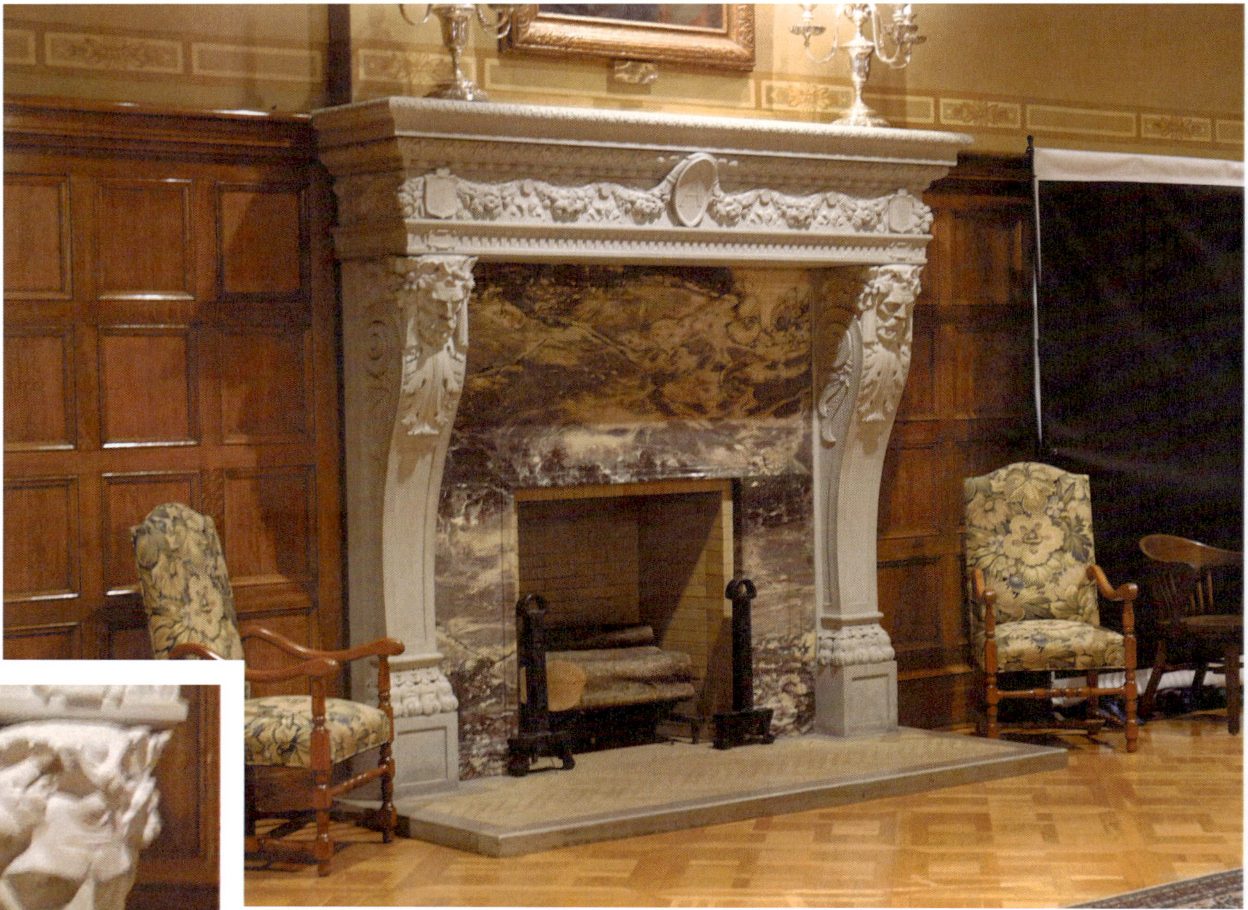

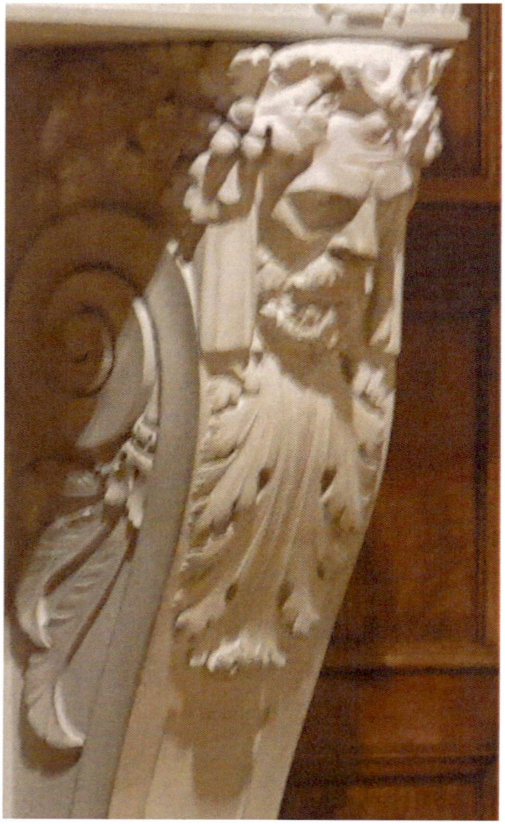

Governor's Reception Hall

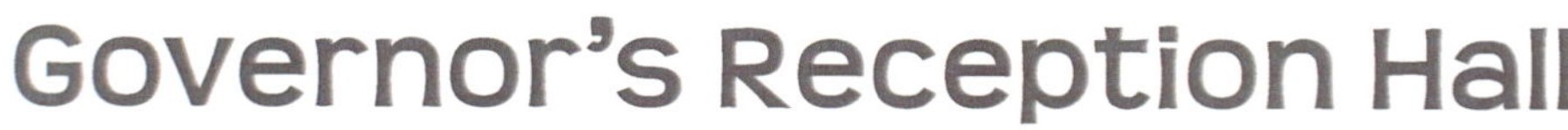

The Governor's Reception Hall is both a public room and the governor's dedicated conference space. Originally decorated with ornate plaster molding, the room's décor was revised by Cass Gilbert to reflect the Craftsman style, emphasizing simple designs and undisguised natural materials.

At each end of the room, Batesville limestone mantels and figured marble inserts surround ornamental fireplaces. The east mantel features carved heads represent the state's historic Native American population; the west mantel's carving call to mind the early European explorers and settlers.

Silver plate chandelier, candelabras and sconces, as well as the rich quarter sawn oak paneling, are original to the room. The wall and ceiling finishes duplicate the 1914-vintage decorative painting.

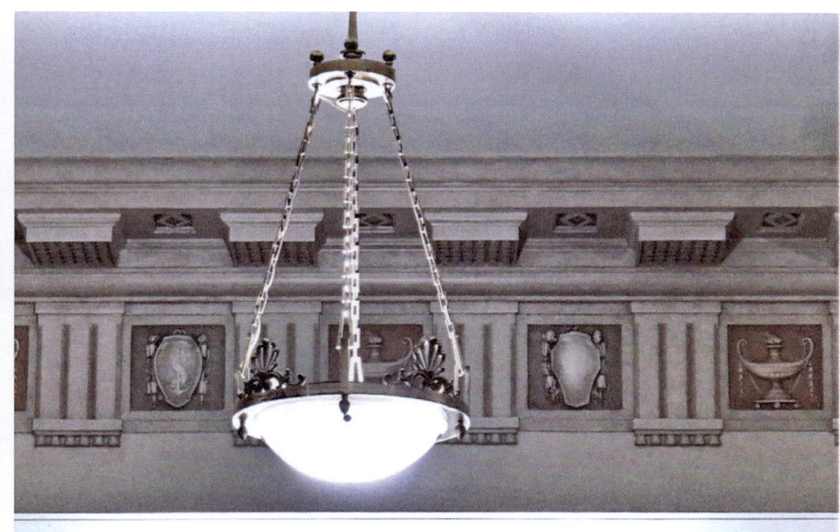

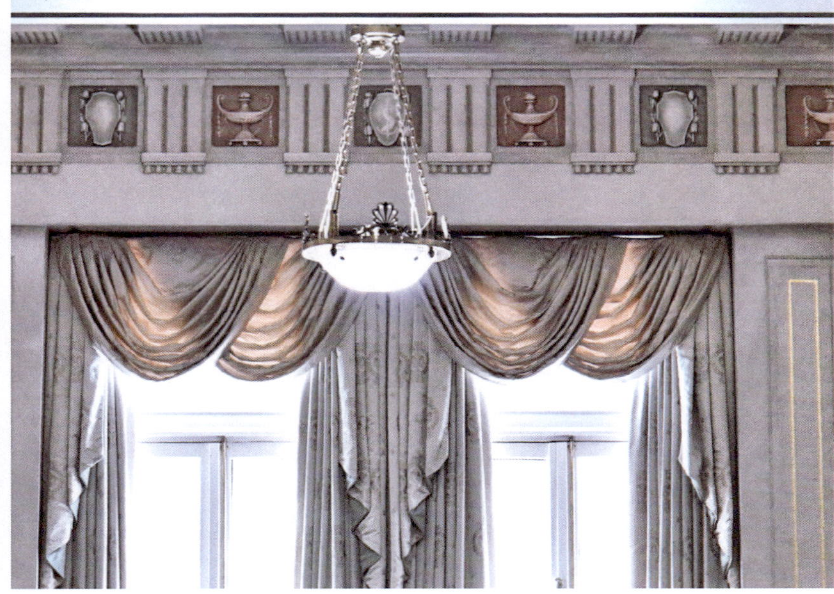

Former Supreme Court Chamber

In 1958, the state Supreme Court relocated to the nearby Justice Building. The court's former chamber is now used as a Senate committee room. However, the filigree still reflects that of a courtroom.

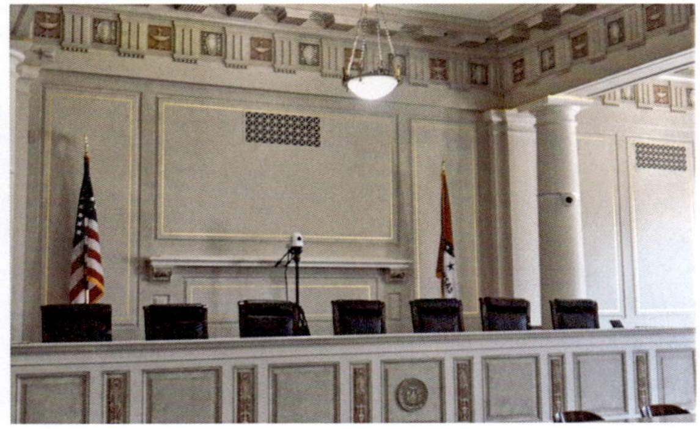

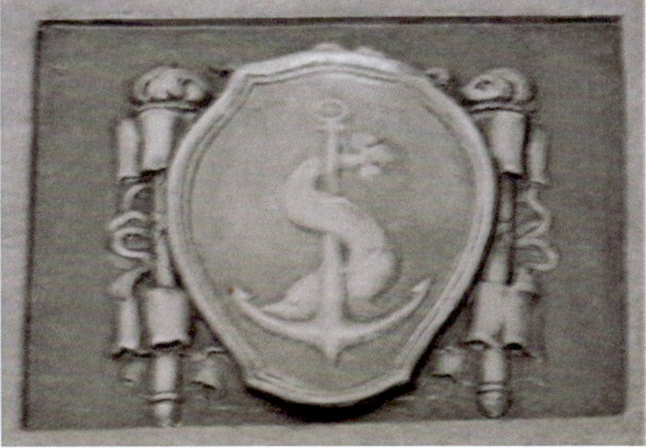

Art Deco Design

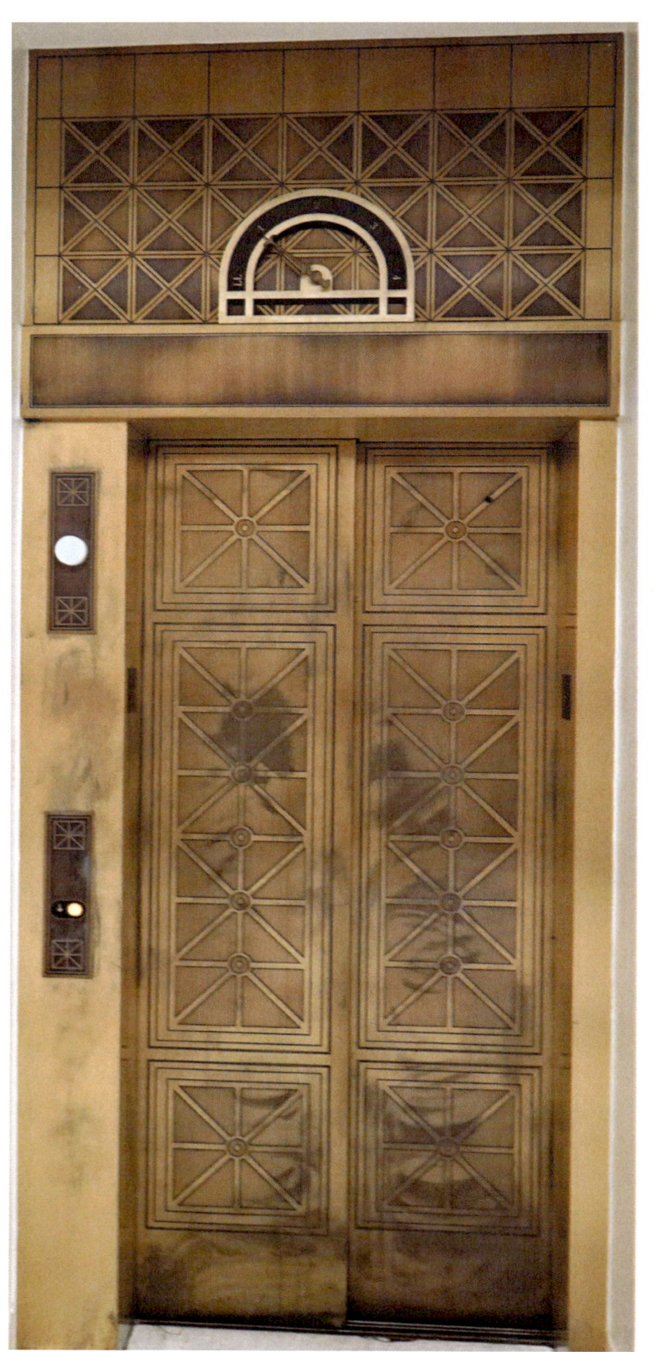

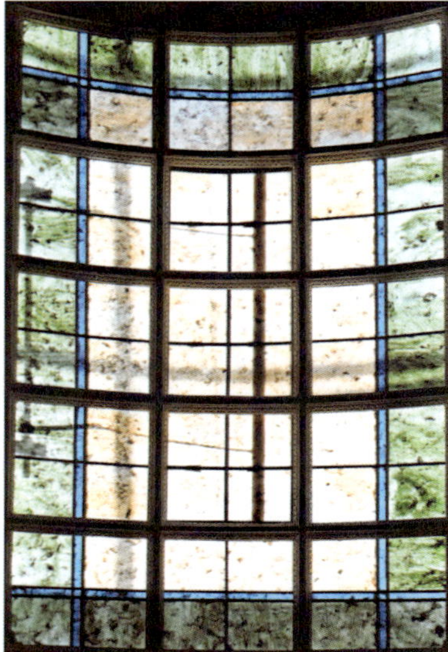

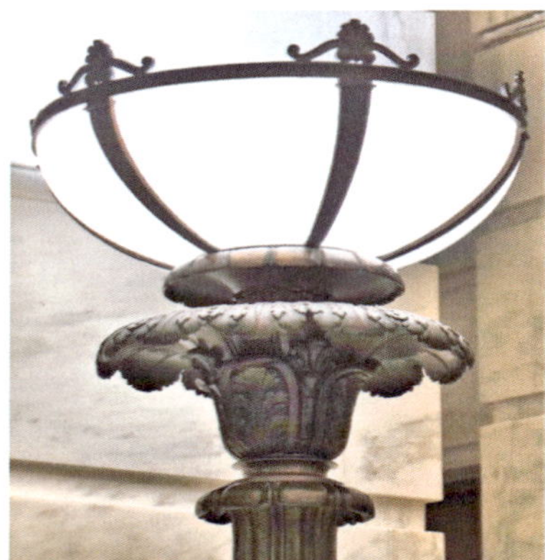

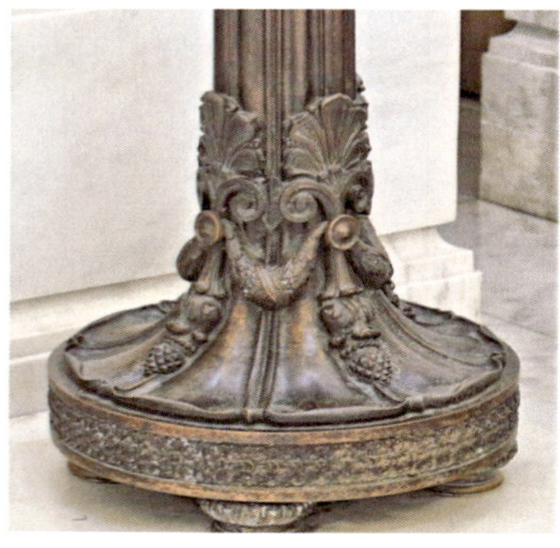

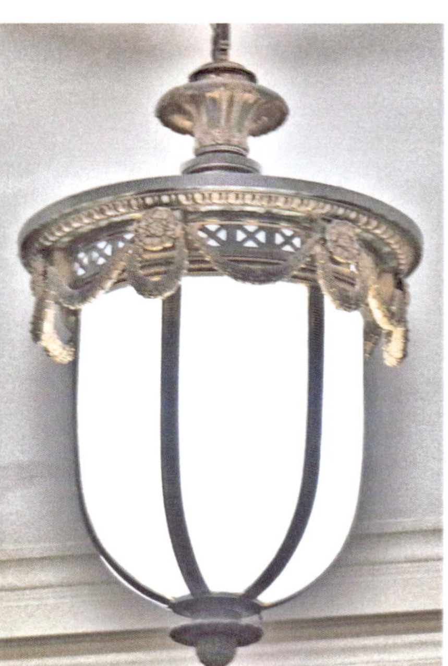

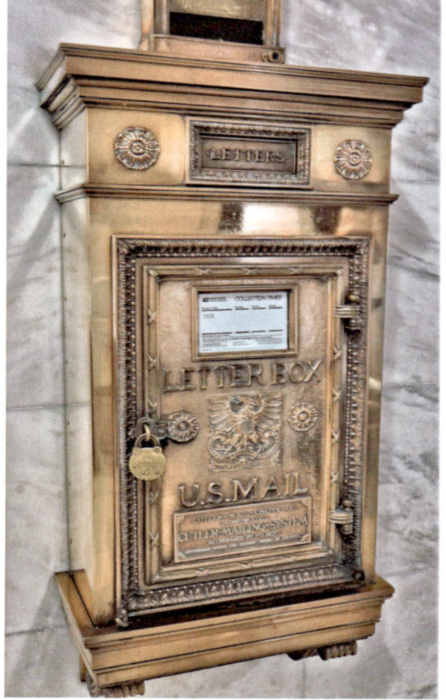

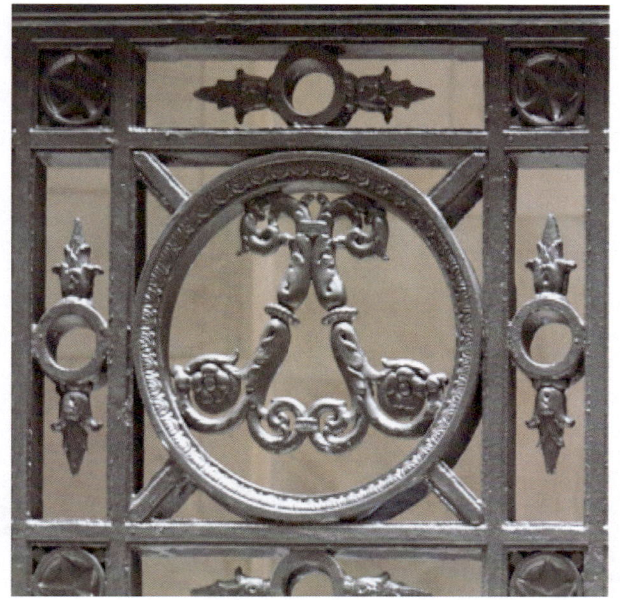

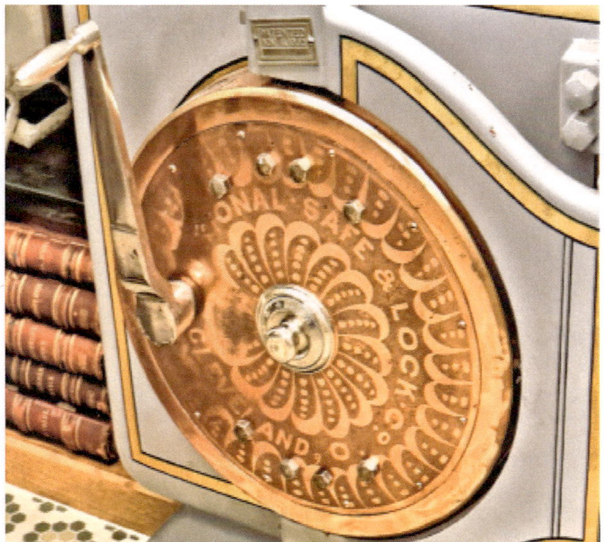

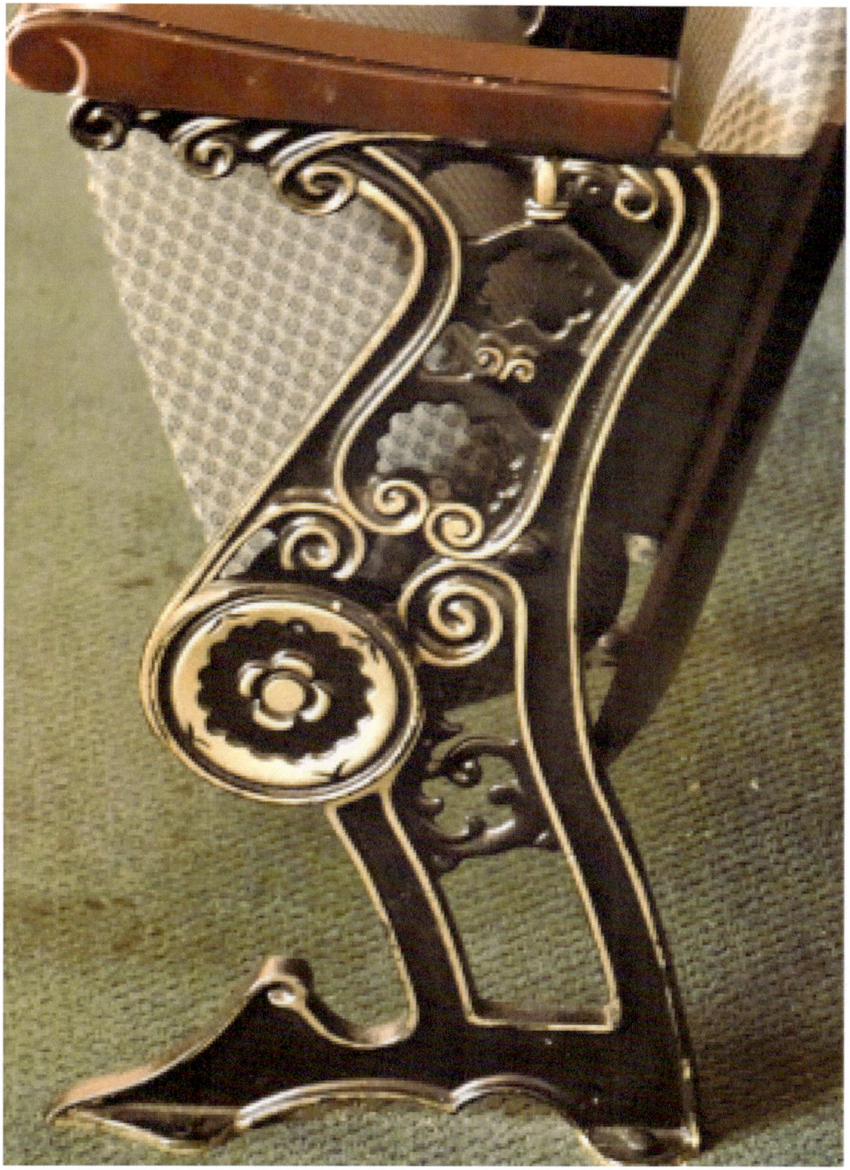

Previous page: Brass elevator doors, stained-glass skylight, brass chandelier, brass lamp, brass mailbox.

Above: Artistic 'A' in railing, theater seats in General Assembly galleries.

Left: Door to vault in state treasury office.

Arkansas State Seal

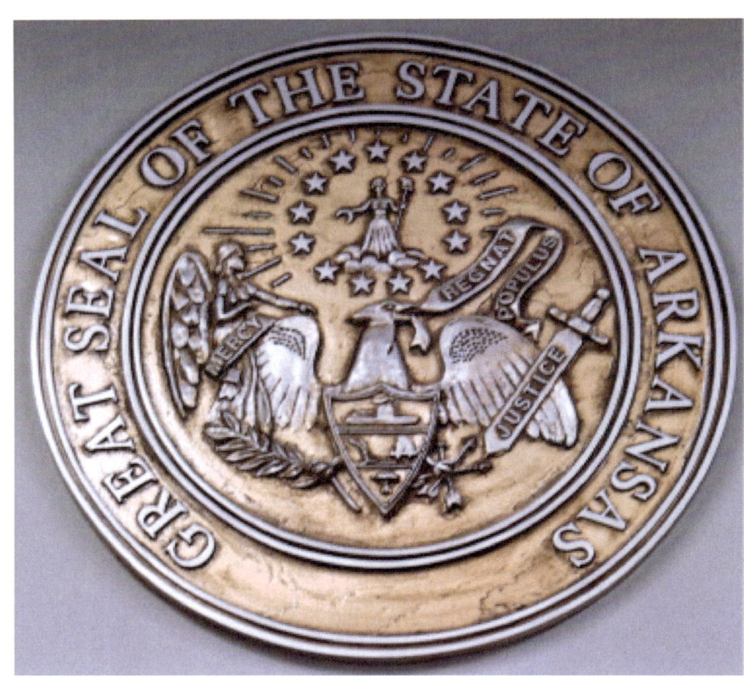

Arkansas' state seal bears the following elements:

  * An eagle at the bottom, holding a scroll in its beak inscribed Regnat Populus, with a bundle of arrows in one claw and an olive branch in the other;

  * A shield covering the breast of the eagle, engraved with a steamboat at the top, a beehive and plow in the middle, and a sheaf of wheat at the bottom;

  * The Goddess of Liberty at the top, holding a wreath in her right hand, a pole in the left hand, surmounted by a liberty cap and surrounded by a circle of stars outside of which is a circle of rays;

  * The figure of an angel on the left, inscribed "Mercy;" and a sword on the right hand, inscribed "Justice."

About the Photographer

Jane Moorman describes herself as an adventurer who loves to drive the back roads to see what there is to see.

During her 30-year journalism career, Jane honed her photographic skills as a photojournalist including covering high school sporting events.

A friend once said, "I wish I could see the world as Jane sees it. Finding the beauty in things that most of us don't take time to see."

Upon retiring in 2021, Jane decided there is a lot of her native country she had not visited, including each state's capitol, so she began her journey of exploring the USA.

She currently lives in Albuquerque, New Mexico, but says her real home is on the road.

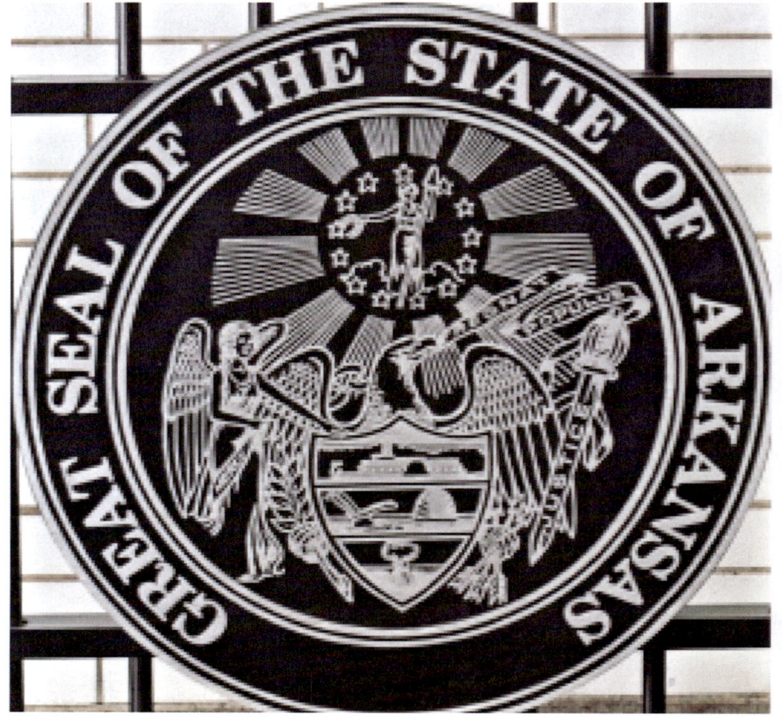